I0814925

MISSION: SPACE SCIENCE

BEYOND THE SOLAR SYSTEM

Sarah Eason

Use Your STEM Skills to Explore Outer Space

Published in 2025 by **Cheriton Children's Books**
1 Bank Drive West, Shrewsbury, Shropshire, SY3 9DJ

First Edition

Author: Sarah Eason
Designers: Paul Myerscough and Steve Mead
Editor: Jennifer Sanderson
Proofreader: Ella Newby
Consultant: David Hawksett, BSc

Picture credits: Cover: Shutterstock/Rdrgraphe (t), Shutterstock/M.Aurelius (b). Inside: p4: Shutterstock/Vadim Sadovski, p5: NASA/Bill Ingalls, p6: Shutterstock/Pike-28, p7: Shutterstock/Marzolino, p8: Shutterstock/Muratart, p9: Wikimedia Commons/Pablo Carlos Budassi, p10b: Wikimedia Commons/Bartolomeu Velho, p10t: Shutterstock/Triff, p11: Wikimedia Commons, p12: NASA/JPL-Caltech/GSFC/JAXA, p13: NASA, p14: NASA/JPL-Caltech, p15: Wikimedia Commons/Roberto Mura, p16: Shutterstock/Triff, p17: NASA/CXC/NGST, p18: Shutterstock/Aphelleon, p19: NASA/STScI/AURA, p20: NASA Goddard, p21: NASA Goddard, p22b: NASA/JPL-Caltech, p22t: NASA/JPL-Caltech/OCIW, p24: NASA/JPL/California Institute of Technology, p25: NASA/JPL-Caltech/SSC, p26: NASA, p27: Dreamstime/Markus Schieder, p28: NASA/JPL-Caltech/GSFC, p29: NASA Goddard, p30b: NASA/ESA/Roi_Levi, p30t: Wikimedia Commons/Johan Hagemeyere, p31: NASA Goddard, p32: ESA p33: Wikimedia Commons/NOIRLab, p34: NASA/JPL-Caltech, p35: NASA/SOFIA/Lynette Cook, p36: NASA, p37: Shutterstock/Dima Zel, p38: NASA, p39: Wikimedia Commons/DOD, p40: NASA/JPL, p41: Shutterstock/IrinaK, p42: NASA/JPL-Caltech, p43: NASA/Ames/JPL-Caltech, p44: NASA/JPL-Caltech/KSC, p45: Shutterstock/Sergey Nivens.

Printed in China

CONTENTS

Chapter 1

LOOKING INTO SPACE

Until about 160 years ago, when gas and electricity lit up our cities, the night skies formed a twinkling blanket over Earth. Compared to the dozens of stars visible to city dwellers today, people long ago would have seen thousands of stars twinkling across the sky on a clear night. However, for thousands of years, they were unaware of the true nature of stars and galaxies.

Our sun is at the center of our solar system, but what lies beyond it?

Making Links

Most ancient cultures made a link between the objects in the sky and their religion. Stars and planets were identified with gods and goddesses, with stories told to explain their movement. People looked for patterns in the stars and named them after heroes and creatures from myths and legends. For example, one constellation represented the hunter Orion to the ancient Greeks. In their stories, he was killed by a giant scorpion. The constellation Scorpius seems to chase Orion across the sky, just as the creature did in the myth.

Watching the Sky

Ancient peoples did not just make up stories about the objects in the sky. They carefully watched and recorded their movements, using them to find their way and to mark the passage of the year. They also hoped to find out what might happen in the future. They believed that the stars could influence conditions on Earth, for example, by causing rain, drought, and plagues.

Eclipses of the sun and moon fascinated ancient people.

SPACE SCIENCE

The Pleiades is a cluster of stars that is named for the seven daughters of Atlas and Pleione. A story says that Orion, the hunter, fell in love with them and chased them, until the god Zeus turned them into doves so they could escape. They flew up into the sky, where they are still seen today.

YOUR MISSION

In this book we will explore beyond the solar system in detail, looking at what we know about outer space and how we learned it. You will also be given thought-provoking space missions to complete that will draw on:

- Your STEM skills: these are science, technology, engineering, and math skills.
- Your social skills: these include identifying skills and strengths in others, team building, persuasive skills, and learning how to work collaboratively.
- Your critical thinking skills: these include being able to evaluate and analyze information, think independently about problems and find solutions, and draw your own conclusions.

All the above skills are vital for successful space exploration—ask any space scientist! So, are you mission-ready? Let's begin the missions and find out.

Ancient Constellations

Astronomers today divide the sky into 88 clearly defined segments known as constellations. Many of these, like Cassiopeia, are based on constellations known since ancient times. Some of the oldest constellations are the 12 that make up the zodiac, including Gemini, Taurus, and Sagittarius. These make up a system that probably dates back to the Babylonian astronomers of nearly 3,000 years ago. The 12 constellations form a circle around the ecliptic, and their positions can be used as a way of navigating. Many different ancient cultures have used the zodiac.

Problems in the Sky

Ptolemy (c. 100—c. 170 CE) was one of the first to try to formalize the constellations. His book, the *Almagest*, described 48 constellations that are still used by astronomers today. But he had a problem: he could not see the whole sky. Different constellations are visible in the Northern and Southern Hemispheres. For example, someone in New York will never be able to see the constellation Crux, better known as the Southern Cross. Likewise, a person in southern Australia will only rarely see Ursa Major.

Crux is a constellation of the southern sky that is centered on four bright stars in a cross shape.

This seventeenth century map of the sky shows constellations and zodiac signs.

Arabic Astronomers

Soon after Ptolemy, Islamic astronomers were able to expand the catalog of constellations with their own observations of stars. They took careful notes of their positions, brightness, and color. Their work was so influential that many of the brightest stars, such as Rigel, Aldebaran, and Betelgeuse, are still referred to by their Arabic names.

Found on Voyages

Still more constellations were defined in the seventeenth and eighteenth centuries. Many of these are seen only in the Southern Hemisphere and had not been visible to the Chinese, Greeks, or Arabs. Explorers such as Pieter Keyser (1540–1596) and Frederick de Houtman (1571–1627) mapped the southern skies while sailing on trading voyages.

SPACE SCIENCE

Many of the most familiar patterns in the night sky are actually asterisms, not constellations. An asterism is a grouping of stars that seems to form a pattern or picture when viewed from Earth. Most of them are part of larger constellations. For example, the "Big Dipper" is an asterism that is part of the larger constellation, Ursa Major.

A Band of Stars

All of the stars we see in the constellations are part of our galaxy, called the Milky Way. If you live in a city, you may not have seen the Milky Way, but if you go somewhere without too much light pollution you will see a dim, glowing band arching across the night sky. The earliest observers disagreed as to what the Milky Way actually was. Some suspected that it was made up of stars, but others, such as the Greek philosopher Aristotle (384–322 BCE), thought that it was caused by the ignition of "exhalations" from stars.

Millions of Stars

Telescopes were invented in the early seventeenth century, and the Italian astronomer Galileo Galilei (1564–1642) soon discovered that the milky band in the sky was actually made up of a huge number of stars. Nearly 150 years later, Immanuel Kant (1724–1804) theorized that the Milky Way might be a flat, rotating disc made up of millions of stars. He was right: the reason it appears as a band across the sky is that we are observing it from our position inside the disc.

The spectacular Milky Way can be seen here above the Giza Pyramids in Egypt, North Africa.

This artist's image shows the Perseus Arm, one of the two major spiral arms of the Milky Way (see below).

A Spiral Shape

In the last century, we have learned much more about our own galaxy. It contains between 100 and 400 billion stars, arranged in a shape called a barred spiral. Our sun (and the solar system that surrounds it) is located on one of the arms of the spiral, called the Orion Arm. The entire Milky Way is about 100,000 light-years in diameter.

SPACE HISTORY

The Milky Way is so-named because it forms a white band across the sky, like spilled milk. "Milky Way" is a direct translation of the Roman name for it, Via Lactea. The Romans took their name from the ancient Greek version, Galaktikos Kyklos. In fact, our word "galaxy" is based on the Greek name for the Milky Way. Some cultures know it by different names; for example, to the Chinese it is the "Silver River."

At the Center

For a very long time, most people believed that Earth was the center of the universe. It makes sense if you try to put yourself in the shoes of people who lived long ago. You cannot feel Earth moving, so how would you know that it rotates on its axis? People long ago thought Earth did not move, so the explanation for the sun rising in the east and moving across the sky to set in the west was that the sun was traveling around Earth, and not the other way around.

This image of Ptolemy's Earth-centered solar system (above) was created in the 1500s. Today, we know that the planets travel around the sun.

Different Movements

Ancient astronomers did know that stars and planets moved differently. The stars seem to rotate around a fixed point high in the sky, but they do not change position relative to each other. The planets, on the other hand, move across the sky, from one constellation in the zodiac to another. Some cultures accounted for this difference by imagining a system where the sun and planets traveled in concentric circles around Earth, while the fixed stars were on the inside of a dome-shaped "lid" that rotated once each day.

Ptolemy's Problem

In the second century CE, Ptolemy's *Almagest* drew on the work of past astronomers to solidify his version of the universe. The moon was seen as orbiting closest to Earth, followed by Mercury and Venus, and then the sun. Beyond that were the other known planets in the correct order. However, it was difficult to make this system match up exactly with the observations of astronomers.

Nicolaus Copernicus made huge strides in understanding our solar system.

A Better Solution

In 1543, Nicolaus Copernicus (1473–1543) published a book that proposed a solution: what if Earth and other planets actually orbited the sun? His system was still not quite right because he thought the planets had circular orbits. They are actually elliptical, and once Johannes Kepler (1571–1630) figured this out, the heliocentric model worked a lot better.

SPACE HISTORY

It took a long time for the heliocentric (sun-centered) model to be accepted. One problem was the Catholic Church, which strongly supported the geocentric (Earth-centered) model. Astronomers such as Galileo were persecuted for supporting heliocentrism.

YOUR MISSION

You have been given the mission of traveling through the Milky Way to find out more about it. What would you hope to learn about the galaxy and its many stars? How do you think studying our own galaxy might help us learn more about other galaxies elsewhere in space?

Chapter 2

LOOKING AT THE STARS

Viewed from Earth, the stars look like beautiful twinkling pinpricks in the sky. However, the reality is very different. For a start, stars are enormous. They are giant, incredibly hot balls of hydrogen and helium, with nuclear reactions taking place in their cores to produce heat and light.

Same at the Start

All stars have more or less the same ratio of elements inside them at the start: about three-quarters hydrogen and one-quarter helium. They also contain small amounts of other, heavier elements, such as oxygen, carbon, and nitrogen. Astronomers collectively call these heavier elements "metals." Depending on where they form and how old they are, stars can have more of these metals. Even so, it is a tiny percentage of the total. Our sun is considered to be a "metal-rich star," but those elements make up fewer than 3 percent of its mass.

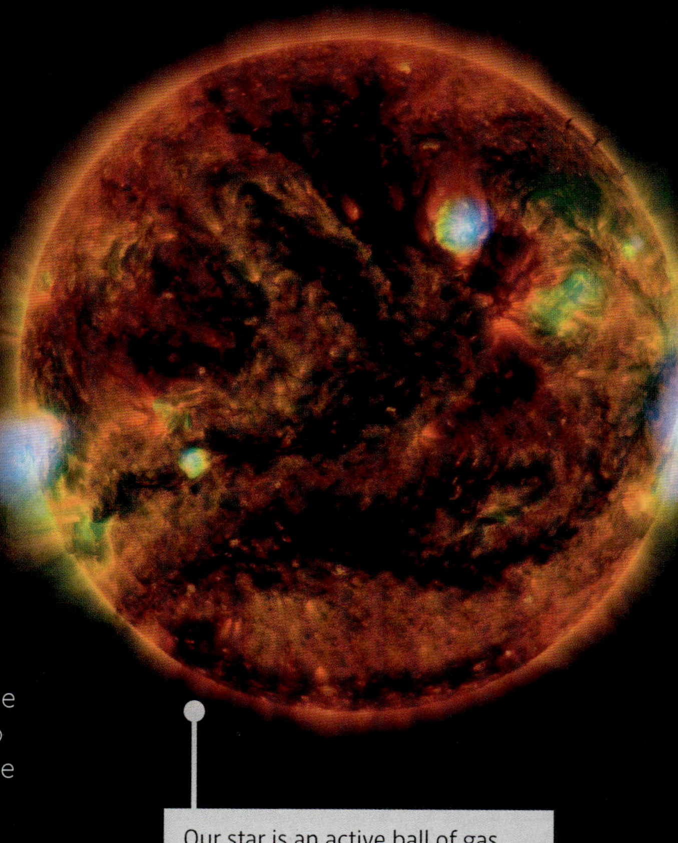

Our star is an active ball of gas. This image of it shows enormous bursts of light on its surface, which are called solar flares.

A Core in Every Star

The structure of stars varies a little, depending on how large they are. However, all stars have a core, which is where the nuclear fusion takes place. The sun is a medium-sized star, and its core takes up about 20 percent of its diameter. Its core is about 170,000 miles (273,588 km) across. The core is the hottest part of a star. Our sun's core is about 27,000,000 degrees Fahrenheit (15,000,000 °C), but a larger star will have a bigger, hotter core.

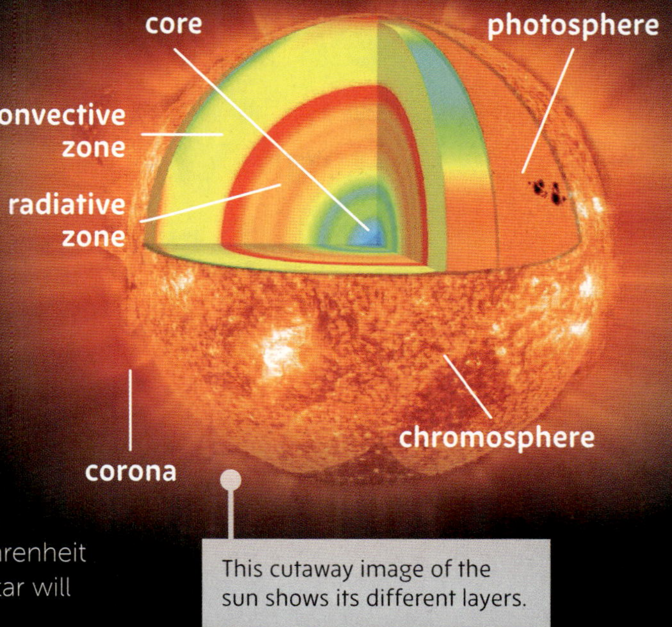

This cutaway image of the sun shows its different layers.

A Lot of Layers

Outside the core is a series of other layers. The convective and radiative zones allow the energy produced in the core to move outward. Outside them is the photosphere. This is the part of the star we see in visible light. Beyond that are the chromosphere and the corona.

Space Science

Inside the core of a star, the temperature and pressure are high enough for nuclear fusion to take place. In a small-to-medium sized star, two hydrogen atoms fuse to form a deuterium atom. Then this merges with another hydrogen atom to create a form of helium. Finally, two of those helium atoms merge to form a different type of helium atom. The process is exothermic, meaning that it releases energy. This energy takes the form of gamma rays that work their way to the surface of the star. During this journey, they change from being gamma rays to being mostly visible light by the time they reach the surface.

This carved-out cloud of gas and dust has been nicknamed the "Jack-o'-lantern Nebula" because it looks like a hollowed-out pumpkin!

Grouping Stars

Astronomers classify stars based on a number of different characteristics. Aside from very young and very old stars (which we will look at later), as a general rule, the bigger a star is, the hotter and brighter it is. There are seven main types of stars: O, B, A, F, G, K, and M. The O and B stars are big and very bright, but fairly rare. At the other end of the scale, M stars are small, dim, and very common. Our sun is a type G star. Big stars can burn incredibly brightly; a type O star might only be 60 times the mass of the sun, but it could still be more than a million times as bright.

Different Colors

Stars can appear to be different colors, based on their surface temperatures. Big stars, such as O and B stars, will appear blue or bluish-white. Small, dim K and M stars will appear orange or red. Our sun is somewhere in the middle—a type of star sometimes called a yellow dwarf.

Unusual Older Stars

Some older stars do not follow the same pattern. For example, the star Betelgeuse, in the constellation of Orion, is a red star, but it is huge, as well as being one of the brightest stars in the sky. It is a type of star called a red supergiant. It has used up the fuel in its core and its outer layers have expanded. As they expand, these older stars become cooler and dimmer, which is why the star appears red instead of blue. Eventually, Betelgeuse will probably explode as a supernova.

Rigel is a blue supergiant star that is found in the constellation of Orion.

SPACE HISTORY

It seems obvious that our sun is a star, but people in ancient times thought the sun and stars were two different types of objects. Seen from Earth, they certainly do not look alike. A few astronomers proposed that stars might be just like the sun, only really far away, but no one took them seriously. It was only in the nineteenth century that someone accurately measured the distance to a star, which allowed us to see that its size and brightness were similar to the sun.

Clues in Energy

The stars are too far away and too hot to visit. Looking at the stars is fascinating, but there are limits to how much we can learn from this, even with the most powerful telescopes available. However, the energy that stars give out comes in many forms, and visible light is only one of them. Astronomers today use all the types of energy to find out more about stars. There are a range of different telescopes, on Earth and in space, which can detect the different types of energy.

Clues in Radio Waves

Stars and other objects in space give off natural radio waves, which can be received by radio telescopes. The precise frequency given off by a star or other object can give clues as to what it is made of. Infrared telescopes pick up the infrared radiation (heat) emitted by objects and dust that cannot be seen by the human eye. Infrared telescopes have been used to find stars being born, as well as planets orbiting other distant stars.

X-ray telescopes can pick up extremely hot objects like stars, and have been used to find black holes. Using an ultraviolet (UV) detector can tell us a lot about a star's chemical makeup, as well as its temperature and density.

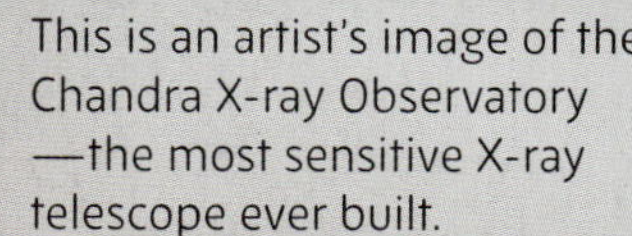

This is an artist's image of the Chandra X-ray Observatory—the most sensitive X-ray telescope ever built.

Telescopes in Space

Since 1990, astronomers have had another useful tool for studying stars. Telescopes in space have a big advantage over telescopes on Earth: they do not have to peer through Earth's thick atmosphere. The gases in our atmosphere can make images blurry and distort other types of signals, and the weather often interferes. Telescopes in space, such as the James Webb Space Telescope, do not have these problems. They have made some amazing discoveries.

SPACE SCIENCE

One of the most useful tools in astronomy is the spectrometer. A spectrometer takes the light collected by a telescope and splits it into its different colors. Astronomers can use this information to find out an object's temperature and mass, and calculate what direction it is moving and how quickly. Spectrometers can even help astronomers figure out what a star is made of.

YOUR MISSION

You are heading up a mission to send an extremely powerful telescope into space to study stars. What types of stars would you be most interested in and why?

Chapter 3

THE LIFE CYCLE OF STARS

This image from the Hubble Space Telescope shows the Ant Nebula—an area in which stars are born.

Stars are not alive in the same way that animals and plants are. However, we often use words such as "birth," "life," and "death" when we talk about stars. This is because they follow a progression that we often call a "life cycle." Over the course of millions or billions of years, stars are formed, they change, and eventually they "die"—an event that can be marked with a slow burning out or a spectacular explosion.

Beginning Life

A star begins its life in a giant cloud of gas and dust called a nebula. These clouds can be hundreds of light-years across, containing enough raw materials to make thousands of stars. These raw materials are mainly hydrogen and helium, with small amounts of heavier elements. The force of gravity pulling in, combined with the force of the molecules pushing out, keeps the nebula in balance.

with another nebula or a star, or a nearby explosion, could make the nebula begin to collapse in on itself. As it collapses, it breaks into smaller and smaller clumps, each with roughly the mass of a star. These clumps of gas start heating up and then form protostars.

All Down to Mass

After that, one of two things could happen. If there is enough mass in the protostar, it can reach temperatures of millions of degrees in its core. This temperature allows the process of nuclear fusion to begin. However, some protostars do not have enough mass to get hot enough for fusion to start. They become what are known as brown dwarfs, and slowly cool down over the next few billion years.

SPACE SCIENCE

Though we often think of space as a vacuum, it is not completely empty. It is made up of an extremely thin mixture of gas and dust that we call the interstellar medium (ISM). It is the ISM that eventually collapses and forms a nebula where stars can form.

This image taken by the Hubble Space Telescope shows a shock wave around a very young star, LL Oricome, indicating a collision.

Stars and Sequences

Once a star begins to release energy, it is known as a main sequence star. A star with a similar mass to our own sun will stay in main sequence for about 10 billion years. During that time, chemical reactions in its core will fuse hydrogen atoms together to form helium, but eventually the star will run out of fuel. When this happens, the core starts to contract and get hotter. Eventually it becomes hot enough for the helium to fuse and form carbon. The star's outer layers expand, and as they expand, they cool down and become less bright. The star is now called a red giant.

Dimming to a Dwarf

When the helium in the core is exhausted, the outer layers of the star drift away. It ends up with a gaseous shell, called a planetary nebula, surrounding the dying core. The core cools and dims, and the star becomes a white dwarf. Eventually it stops shining and is then called a black dwarf. The universe is not yet old enough for any white dwarfs to have cooled into black dwarfs.

This image shows an enormous bubble being blown into space by a superhot, massive star within the Bubble Nebula.

A Different Path

Stars with significantly more mass than our sun follow a different path after they reach main sequence. Although they have a lot more fuel than smaller stars, they use it up much more quickly. Once this happens, the star becomes a red supergiant, with a helium core surrounded by a shell of cooling, expanding gas. In the core, chemical reactions create heavier and heavier elements, until the star can no longer extract any energy from the process. Its own gravity causes it to collapse, and the core heats up to billions of degrees Fahrenheit before exploding in a supernova. The explosion sends huge amounts of energy and matter out into space.

The explosions produced by supernovae are so brilliant that dying stars can appear to shine as brightly as an entire galaxy.

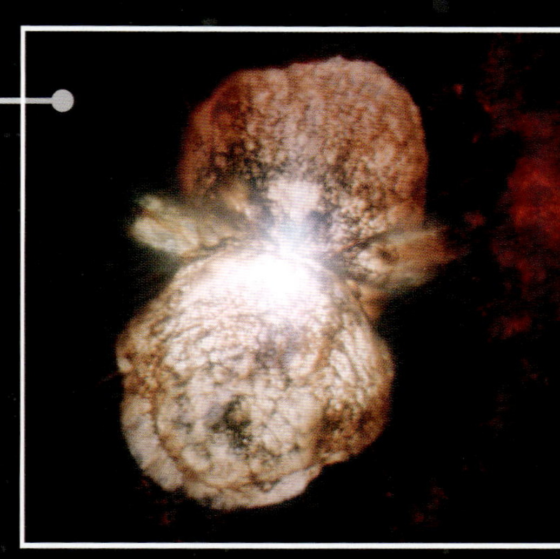

Space Science

When a dying star explodes, it leaves behind the remains of its core. Depending on how massive the original star was, this core can turn into either a neutron star or a black hole. Both of these objects are extremely dense. A single teaspoon full of a neutron star's material, for example, would weigh about 1.1 billion tons (1 billion mt)!

Young, hot blue stars lie in the outer spiral arms of galaxy NGC 300, while older stars fill the yellow-green center.

Expanding Knowledge

In the past 40 years or so, improvements in technology and the launch of several space telescopes have meant that our knowledge of stars has grown by leaps and bounds. In addition to returning amazing images of nebulae, explosions from dying giant stars called supernovae, and distant galaxies, these telescopes are allowing astronomers to peer into the farthest corners of the universe. They are finding some amazing things.

Stars with Tails

In 2007, astronomers scanning the universe for UV light discovered that a well-known star, named Mira, actually has a long tail, like a comet. Mira is a red giant, an older star that is starting to lose its surface material. As it hurtles through space, this tail, made up of carbon, oxygen, and other elements, streams out behind it.

A close-up view of Mira racing through space faster than a speeding bullet can be seen in this image.

An Ancient Star

In 2014, a team of researchers in Australia discovered that one star was older than any other known star. It is in the Milky Way galaxy, only about 6,000 light-years from Earth, and the astronomers estimate that it is 13.6 billion years old—nearly as old as the universe itself. They were able to date it by scanning to see how much iron was present in the star. The older the star, the less iron it has.

A Giant Star

A second discovery in 2014 was of the largest yellow star discovered—one of the 10 largest stars we know of. Its diameter is between 1,100 and 1,600 times larger than the sun's, and it is part of a double star system.

SPACE SCIENCE

The farthest known galaxy is more than 13 billion light-years away. This means that it takes 13 billion years for its light to reach us. To put it another way, the light that astronomers are seeing now was actually emitted 13 billion years ago.

YOUR MISSION

Traveling by spacecraft to the farthest known galaxy is currently impossible—it is more than 13 billion light-years away. If you were tasked with creating a means of travel that could take you to that galaxy, what form might that take? What key characteristics would you look for when selecting astronauts for the mission? And if you were successful, what would be your key objectives for the mission?

Chapter 4

DISCOVERING GALAXIES

Up until the 1920s, almost all astronomers believed that all the stars in the universe were contained in the Milky Way. However, since the invention of telescopes, astronomers had been cataloging what they called "nebulae," meaning "clouds." These objects might appear star-like to the naked eye, but through a telescope they are fuzzy and indistinct. A few astronomers speculated that some of these nebulae might actually be other galaxies, too far away to see clearly. The astronomers were right.

The Andromeda galaxy is the biggest galaxy in the group nearest to us, which includes our Milky Way.

Helpful Hubble

Now we know—or at least, we can estimate—that there are between 100 billion and 200 billion galaxies in the universe. Since its launch in 1990, the Hubble Space Telescope has proven to be extremely useful at finding galaxies. In 2004, the telescope took a million-second exposure in a small area of the constellation Fornax. Astronomers were able to count 10,000 galaxies in the resulting image.

Looking Again

In 2012, they looked again at a narrower portion of the field, but this time using upgraded instruments, and found even more galaxies. Galaxies are not spread randomly throughout the universe; they clump together in groups. The Milky Way is part of a group of several dozen galaxies known as the Local Group.

In turn, this group is part of the Virgo Supercluster, which contains at least 100 groups and clusters of galaxies. In 2014, scientists discovered that even the Virgo Supercluster is part of a much larger grouping, the Laniakea Supercluster. All of its galaxies are being pulled toward a patch of space called the Great Attractor.

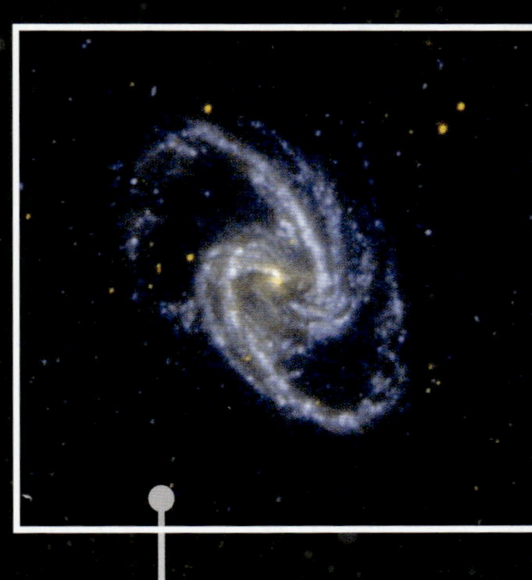

This image shows galaxy NGC 1365, which is part of the Fornax cluster of galaxies.

Space Science

The closest galaxy to the Milky Way is actually inside it! In 2003, astronomers discovered the Canis Major Dwarf Galaxy by analyzing infrared images of the Milky Way. These images showed the cool red M-type stars of Canis Major, which would otherwise be hard to see. At one point in the distant past, the Milky Way swallowed up the smaller galaxy, and now its stars are part of the Milky Way.

Many Different Shapes and Sizes

Galaxies come in a huge range of sizes: the smallest dwarf galaxies may have only a few thousand stars, while the largest galaxies contain an estimated 100 trillion stars. On this scale, the Milky Way falls in the middle, with anywhere from 100 to 400 billion stars. Galaxies also come in a range of different shapes. The three basic galaxy shapes are elliptical, spiral, and irregular.

Messier 96 is a spiral galaxy just over 35 million light-years away. It is about the same size as the Milky Way.

Squished, Circular, and Flattened

Elliptical galaxies are shaped like slightly squished spheres. From Earth, since we can see them in only two dimensions, they look like oval discs. They appear brightest at the center, then gradually become dimmer the farther out you go. They are classified based on how squished they are. An E0 galaxy is nearly a perfect circle. At the other end of the scale, an E7 galaxy is flattened.

Spiral Galaxies

A spiral galaxy has a bulge at the center, surrounded by a flat disc, a little like Saturn and its rings. The bulge at the center is made up mainly of older stars, and the disc contains younger stars, along with a lot of gas and dust. The arm shapes in the disc give spiral galaxies their name. Some spiral galaxies are called "barred spirals." In a barred spiral galaxy, like the Milky Way, the arms do not come out directly from the central bulge. Instead, there is a straight bar running through the center of the galaxy, and the arms come out from that.

An Irregular Group

The last type of galaxy is an irregular galaxy. These have a lot of gas and dust but no particular shape or structure, and they make up an estimated one-quarter of all galaxies. Some irregular galaxies probably used to be spiral or elliptical, but they were deformed by gravity from other galaxies or from colliding and merging with other galaxies.

SPACE SCIENCE

A fourth type of galaxy, the lenticular galaxy, is really just a halfway point between an elliptical galaxy and a spiral galaxy. These galaxies have a central bulge and a thin disc, like a spiral galaxy, but they have no spiral structure. They are shaped a little like a lens, which is how they get their name.

Some galaxies, like this spiral galaxy below, contain trillions of stars.

A Black Hole

Astronomers believe that at the center of nearly all galaxies, including the Milky Way, there is a black hole. A black hole is not really a hole: holes are empty, and black holes are not empty. They are areas where there is a huge amount of matter squished into a very small space. Since they are so incredibly dense, they exert a huge gravitational field. It is so strong that nothing can escape it.

An enormous jet of bright matter is shown at the center of this black hole, known as a blazer.

Made by a Dying Star

Most black holes are formed when a massive star dies. Our sun is not big enough to turn into a black hole, but a much bigger star, such as Betelgeuse, will explode in a supernova after it uses up its fuel. Part of the dying star is blasted off into space, and the remainder collapses under the force of its own gravity to form a black hole. These are known as stellar mass black holes.

Enormous Black Holes

The black holes at the center of the galaxies are much bigger—so much bigger in fact, they are called supermassive black holes. They have a mass of more than 1 million suns. Astronomers are trying to figure out how supermassive black holes form. One recent theory is that they start out small, but grow and grow as more matter falls into them.

A Difficult Task

Studying black holes is extremely tricky—nothing, not even light, can escape them, so we have no way to "see" them. We cannot even use x-rays or other forms of energy to see them. However, we can infer their presence by looking for their effect on other nearby objects. For example, if a star or cloud of gas and dust passes near a black hole, its matter will be drawn toward the black hole.

This simulation image shows two stars colliding and joining to form a black hole. This is one theory about how black holes may form.

Space Science

Black holes are surrounded by a boundary known as the event horizon. Once something falls inside the event horizon, it can never escape. Even time is distorted near the event horizon. To an outside observer, something falling into the black hole would appear to move more and more slowly, but never reach it.

Understanding the Universe

In the first half of the twentieth century, scientists wrestled with the concept of the universe. Has it always been there, or was there a time when it did not exist? Does it go on forever, or does it have an edge somewhere? These are difficult questions to answer, and we still do not know for sure. Improved technology has helped scientists get closer to the answers.

Making Breakthroughs

One of the key breakthroughs was the discovery that galaxies do not stand still in space. In the 1920s, the astronomer Edwin Hubble (1889–1953) studied the spectra of light coming from distant galaxies. Objects that are moving away from us emit light that is shifted toward the red end of the spectrum. This phenomenon is a result of the Doppler Effect, the same thing that makes an ambulance's siren sound more high-pitched as it approaches you. The farther away a galaxy is, the more its light is red-shifted.

Edwin Hubble helped later astronomers make even greater discoveries about the universe.

Galaxy mergers can occur when two or more galaxies collide and join (see opposite).

Getting Bigger and Bigger

Based on Hubble's discovery that galaxies are moving away from each other, astronomers concluded that the universe must be expanding. It is a little like a loaf of raisin bread rising in the oven: as it rises, the raisins (like galaxies) are caught up in the expanding dough and move away from each other. If the universe is expanding, then it must have been much smaller at some point in the past. That led to the concept of the Big Bang: the idea that the universe began as a single point before expanding rapidly.

Big Bang Leftovers

In 1963, a pair of astronomers discovered microwave radiation coming equally from all directions. The astronomers first thought something was wrong with their antenna, but then realized that this was background radiation left over from the Big Bang. Scientists have studied this radiation to learn more about how the universe formed.

SPACE SCIENCE

Although many galaxies are moving away from each other, the Milky Way and the Andromeda galaxy are actually moving toward each other. The huge force of the gravitational attraction between them is stronger than the force of the universe expanding. They will collide in about 4 billion years.

This illustration shows the merger between our Milky Way galaxy and its neighbor the Andromeda galaxy.

YOUR MISSION

To date, it has been impossible to reach a black hole, because the nearest is so far away. And if any equipment did enter a black hole, it would be destroyed. But imagine if it were possible for either a manned spacecraft or a probe to enter a black hole and survive, and to send back data about what was discovered there. What would you hope to learn if you were in charge of such a mission?

Chapter 5

MYSTERIES OF OUTER SPACE

There is a lot about the universe that we still do not understand, and new discoveries are always being made. One of the most useful of discoveries was the existence of pulsars. In 1967, astronomers Jocelyn Bell (b. 1943) and Antony Hewish (1924–2021) picked up a mysterious radio emission from a point in the sky. It peaked every 1.33 seconds precisely. This sort of regularity is unusual, and some scientists thought it was communication from an intelligent life form.

Spinning Stars

Additional discoveries confirmed that Bell and Hewish had discovered the first pulsar. A pulsar is created after a supernova, when the exploding star does not have enough mass to become a black hole. Instead, the remains of the supernova collapse to form a neutron star. This neutron star is small and very dense, and when it starts to spin rapidly, it sends out powerful blasts of radiation, but only along the lines of its magnetic field.

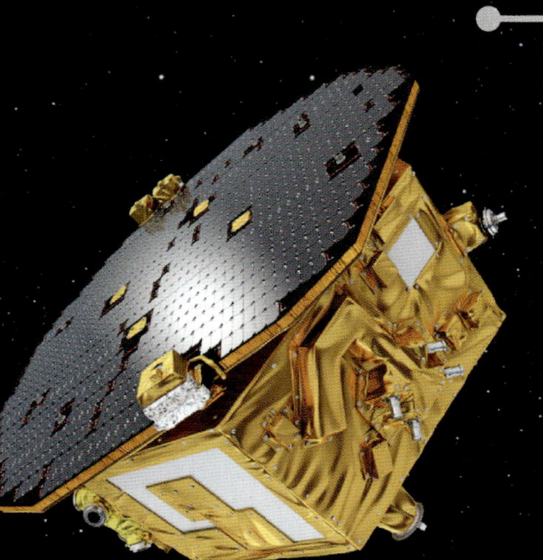

This artist's image shows the Pathfinder spacecraft on its mission to detect gravitational waves in space (see opposite).

Growing Quieter

More recent discoveries have shown that pulsars have a limited life span. They start off spinning incredibly quickly, but as they release more and more energy through their beams, they start to slow down. After 10 to 100 million years, a pulsar will slow down enough that its beams shut off, and it becomes a quiet, regular neutron star.

This artist's image illustrates the concept of gravitational waves, shown rippling outward through space as they pass through objects such as planets.

Perfect Timing

Pulsars are incredibly useful to astronomers. They spin with such regularity that they can be used as timers. They are also used to search for things called gravitational waves, which are like ripples in the fabric of space-time. When they pass through an object, these ripples make it shrink or stretch by a tiny amount. A group of scientists has recently proposed using the signals from pulsars as a type of universal GPS system for spacecraft navigating beyond our solar system or anywhere in our galaxy.

Bell and Hewish did not really believe that the signal they found was a message from another civilization, but they did consider the possibility. They named the signal LGM-1, which stood for "Little Green Men."

Mysterious Objects

The mystery of quasars started in the 1960s, when astronomers looking at radio waves from stars found several small, incredibly bright objects that they could not explain. They called them quasi-stellar radio sources—"quasars" for short—and tried to find out what they were.

Arguing Astronomers

Over the next 20 years or so, astronomers argued over different theories about quasars. Some quasars were shown to be moving away from us at extremely fast speeds. Some were emitting as much light as an entire galaxy. Astronomers wondered if they could be caused by a black hole distorting gravity, or if they could be one end of a wormhole.

Astronomers using the National Aeronautics and Space Administration (NASA) Spitzer and Chandra space telescopes have discovered swarms of quasars in dusty galaxies in the distant universe.

Coming to an Agreement

In the 1980s, astronomers began to agree that quasars were related to what is called an active galactic nucleus (AGN). Nucleus is just another word for the center of a galaxy, and some galaxies have centers that are active, meaning that they emit large amounts of radiation. The radiation can take the form of radio waves, visible light, x-rays, gamma rays, and more. The radiation is also highly variable. This means that it can change intensity in a short amount of time.

Massive Black Holes

The best explanation for quasars seems to be that they are supermassive black holes at the centers of some galaxies. As material is pulled into the black hole, it heats up to incredibly high temperatures and emits large amounts of energy, and it is this energy that we see. When there is no matter "feeding" the black hole, the jets of energy shut down. There is no matter entering the supermassive black hole at the center of the Milky Way, so our galaxy does not appear as a quasar.

A thick ring of dust can surround the huge activity at the center of a supermassive black hole.

Space Science

A quasar can easily be 100 times brighter than the host galaxy that surrounds it. As a result of this, we cannot take an image that shows both the quasar and the host galaxy—the galaxy is lost in the quasar's glare. It is only fairly recently that photographic technology has improved to the point where we can now detect a big enough range of brightnesses in a single image.

All objects in the universe, from stars to planets, are attracted to each other because of the force of gravity.

Holding the Milky Way Together

Understanding gravity is important to understanding how the entire universe works. All objects with mass are attracted—through the force of gravity—to other objects. The greater the mass, the stronger the pull. It is gravity that keeps Earth in orbit around the sun and holds the Milky Way together.

Matter We Cannot See

Astronomers soon noticed a problem with gravity: there did not seem to be enough mass around to exert the gravitational force that could be observed. In the 1930s, an astronomer named Fritz Zwicky (1898–1974) was studying a far-off cluster of galaxies when he realized that if the only mass in the cluster was the galaxies themselves, then they were moving too fast for that amount of gravity to hold them together. He decided that there must be a lot of additional matter that we cannot see because it does not emit light.

Truth of the Darkness

Since then, scientists have tried to figure out the truth behind dark matter, and there are a lot of theories but no firm answers. There is evidence that the amount of dark matter in the universe is a lot higher than the amount of matter we can see. Other evidence shows that dark matter cannot be made up of protons and neutrons, like the matter we know of. It could be made up of a type of particle that we have not yet discovered.

Searching for Answers

Several projects searching for dark matter are underway. Some scientists are working on designing new types of detection tools that will allow them to detect dark matter particles. Other studies focus on detecting the effects of dark matter, for example, by looking for x-rays or gamma rays being given off when dark matter particles decay. Others collide beams of high-energy protons to look for dark matter particles.

Space Science

In 1998, data from the Hubble Space Telescope showed that the expansion of the universe is accelerating. This surprised scientists, who thought that the force of gravity would slow it down. One theory to explain acceleration is that the universe is full of something called "dark energy," which has the opposite effect of gravity, pulling galaxies apart.

The Hubble Space Telescope travels 353 miles (569 km) above Earth's surface, where it can clearly see objects in space.

YOUR MISSION

Imagine you have been charged with a mission to study dark matter. During the mission, you discover things about space that are in direct conflict with current theories. How would you present that information to other scientists, and the world? The early scientist Galileo faced outrage when he first suggested that the sun and not Earth was at the center of our solar system. Do you think you would face a similar reaction today if you challenged current beliefs? Why or why not?

Chapter 6

ALWAYS MORE MISSIONS

Modern technology and tools such as space telescopes are redefining astronomy, leading to an incredible expansion in what we know about the universe. Even so, there are so many questions that remain unanswered, including what is dark matter and is there intelligent life anywhere out there?

Finding Out More and More

New discoveries have come thick and fast. Data from the Planck space telescope showed that the universe is older than we had thought. This means that space and time are not expanding quite as fast as scientists had estimated. A team of scientists have discovered a record-breaking cluster of quasars stretching 4 billion light-years across. Researchers have also found the first direct evidence for the dramatic expansion just after the Big Bang.

The James Webb Telescope is collecting data in space that will help us learn more about the universe and dark matter.

A Good Way to Spend Money?

Despite these discoveries, many people question why we spend so much time, effort, and money studying things that are billions of light-years away. For example, it cost around $10 billion to get the James Webb Space Telescope into orbit. With all of the problems our planet faces, some people wonder if that money could be better spent closer to home.

Big Advantages

The truth is that research into space has benefits on Earth. Many technologies developed for astronomy have a number of other very useful applications. A good example is the charge-coupled device that made cameras in early smartphones work, but was originally developed for astronomy imaging. GPS satellites rely on quasars and distant galaxies to determine their position and help you find your way, and a computer language designed to control a telescope is used to track packages during shipping.

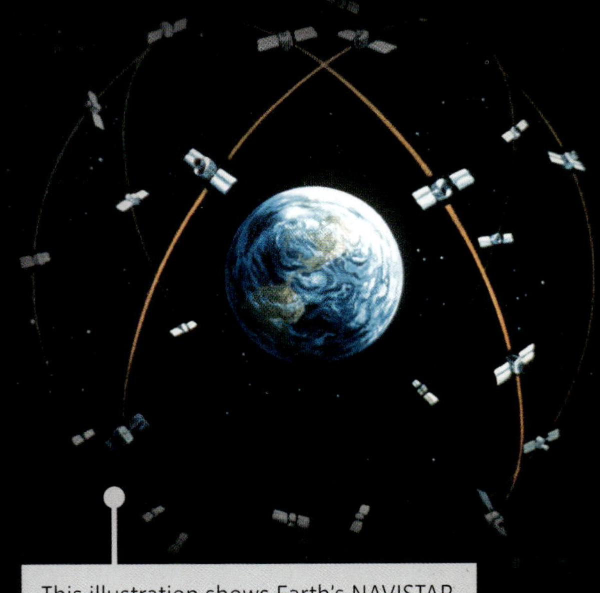

This illustration shows Earth's NAVISTAR GPS system. Systems such as this would not be possible without space research.

SPACE SCIENCE

Many arguments about money spent on astronomy miss out on the key thing driving most astronomers—the need to find answers. It is human nature to ask questions about how the universe was created and where we came from. With advances in technology, we are getting closer to being able to answer those questions.

has been carried out over the years by government agencies, universities, and private companies. One of the main methods has been analyzing radio waves from outside the solar system.

Artificial Signals

Our own civilization emits a lot of radiation through things like television broadcasts. The signals are easy to recognize as being artificial, and if we could find similar signals coming from space, it might be a sign of intelligent life. One new technique is using telescopes to search for alien laser signals. Lasers are a way of transmitting messages over huge distances, but the signals would be incredibly faint by the time they reached Earth.

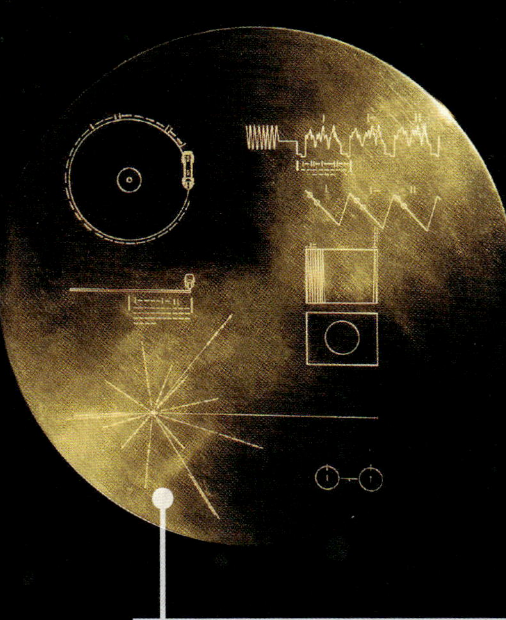

Copies of this golden record have been carried into space on the Voyager probes. They contain important information about humans and Earth—information that could lead extraterrestrial life straight toward us!

The Very Large Array is an observation area in southwestern United States that gathers data about space. Could it one day tell us that we are not alone?

Should We Keep Quiet?

If there is intelligent life elsewhere in the universe, these beings may be conducting their own version of SETI. What would happen if they found us? Some scientists have speculated that if an alien civilization is more advanced than ours, it might be able to destroy us. After all, in Earth's own history, when two cultures have met for the first time, the less-advanced culture has often been harmed. Some scientists think we should "lie low," and not try to alert other civilizations to our presence.

SPACE SCIENCE

Life on Earth has evolved to take advantage of the conditions on our home planet. For example, all life we know of requires water, and there is plenty of water on Earth. Plants and animals are adapted to the fairly narrow range of temperatures found on Earth. However in alien worlds, with other conditions, life might look very different.

Speeding up the Search

One thing that could speed up the search for intelligent life is the discovery of planets orbiting distant stars. They are called exoplanets or extrasolar planets, and they are being discovered at an amazing rate. Since the first one was found in 1992, they have been popping up everywhere, and at the last count there were more than 5,000 of them. These exoplanets are too far away for us to visit with current technology, but in the distant future, we may be able to colonize them.

Gravity's Pull

Planets do not emit light, and compared to stars, they are incredibly small, so we cannot directly see them with telescopes. One way to find exoplanets is by looking for tiny changes in a star's velocity, which are caused by the planet's gravity pulling at them. This technique is most useful for finding massive gas giants similar to Jupiter. Another technique is to look for changes in a star's light. If a planet passes in front of a star, it will block some of the light and make the star appear dimmer. This is how the Kepler space telescope found exoplanets.

Finding Out More

Finding an exoplanet is just the first step. Astronomers need to then find out what it is made of, and whether it has things like an atmosphere or liquid water. One way of doing this is to study the exoplanet through the infrared portion of the electromagnetic spectrum, looking for chemical signatures of different elements. An experiment using the Keck Observatory in Hawaii was able to use spectroscopy to identify a number of water molecules in the atmosphere of one exoplanet.

The exoplanet 55 Cancri e likely has an atmosphere thicker than Earth's, but similar. The planet is so close to its star that one side constantly faces it, resulting in a dayside and a nightside.

This is an artist's image of the Kepler space telescope. Perhaps it will soon discover many more exoplanets, and life there too!

SPACE SCIENCE

Astronomers can gauge how habitable a planet might be by seeing how far it is from the star it orbits. If it is too close, the surface would be too hot, and any liquid water would evaporate into space. If it is too far away, it would be too cold, and the water would freeze. If a planet falls in the "just right" area—often called the Goldilocks zone—it is more likely to have liquid water on the surface.

YOUR MISSION

You have been tasked with the mission of analyzing the risks and benefits of searching for extraterrestrial life, and presenting your findings to NASA and other space organizations. Draw up a list of the risks and benefits, then give your conclusion: do you think there is more to gain or more to lose through missions to find extraterrestrials?

CONCLUSION
FUTURE MISSIONS

In 2013, an amazing milestone was reached when the Voyager 1 probe left the solar system behind and traveled into interstellar space. It was the very first humanmade object ever to leave the solar system, and was followed in 2018 by its partner, Voyager 2. Both probes are still sending back data about the conditions they encounter on their voyage into the universe.

Next Big Breakthroughs

As a result of the huge distances involved, the next breakthroughs in the study of the universe will come from telescopes on Earth, or from those in orbit around it. We have had great results from the Hubble, Spitzer, and Kepler space telescopes, as well as the Chandra X-ray Observatory. The James Webb Space Telescope, which uses infrared radiation, was launched into space in 2021.

Voyager 1 was launched in 1977. It is still journeying into outer space, gathering data that can help us discover even more about the universe.

Dark Matter, Dark Energy, and Much More

Scientists are currently investigating a huge range of topics. Research into new technologies is keeping pace, bringing telescopes and other tools that are much more sensitive than before. The search for dark matter and dark energy continues, and there are many studies looking at energy that will give us clues to conditions just after the Big Bang. Since the launch of the Kepler mission, the study of exoplanets has become a very popular area of research. There is still a lot to be learned, even within our own galaxy.

YOUR FUTURE MISSION

Perhaps this book has inspired you to find out more about our solar system and other solar systems in space. Maybe, one day, you'll even carve out a career in space science and make it your mission to explore the mysteries of the universe and unlock its secrets.

GLOSSARY

asterisms groups of stars that appear to make a shape or pattern when seen from Earth

atmosphere the layer of gases surrounding a planet or moon

atoms the smallest possible units of a chemical element. Atoms are the basis of all matter in the universe

constellation a recognizable pattern of stars that makes up one of the 88 regions of the sky designated by astronomers

dark matter a type of matter that is believed to exist, cannot be seen, but still exerts a gravitational force

ecliptic the apparent path of the sun, as seen from Earth against the background stars

elliptical shaped like a slightly squished circle

galaxies groups of billions of stars and other matter held together by gravity

gamma rays high-energy electromagnetic radiation. Some objects in space produce gamma rays

gravity the force that pulls all objects toward each other

infrared radiation electromagnetic energy with a long wavelength, and cannot be seen as visible light

light-years units of distance equal to the distance light can travel in one year, about 6 trillion miles (9.46 trillion km)

mass a measure of how much matter is in an object

microwave a type of high-frequency radio wave. It can be used to send data over long distances

nebula a cloud of gas and dust in space. Stars are formed in some nebulae

neutron star a small, incredibly dense type of star that forms during a supernova

nuclear fusion a chemical process in which the nuclei of two or more atoms fuse into a more massive nucleus. This process releases a huge amount of energy

orbiting following a curved path around an object in space, such as a moon orbiting a planet

particle one of the tiniest units of matter we know of. Atoms are made up of particles such as protons, neutrons, and electrons

pulsars types of rapidly rotating neutron stars that send out regularly timed pulses of energy

quasars objects found in the centers of some galaxies that emit huge amounts of energy

radiation waves of energy sent out by sources of heat or light, such as the sun. Radiation can be harmful to living things

radio waves very low-frequency types of electromagnetic waves

spectrometer a tool used for measuring wavelengths of light by spreading radiation into an ordered sequence

universe all matter and energy that exists

UV light a type of electromagnetic energy with a short wavelength, which cannot be seen as visible light

x-ray a type of very high-energy electromagnetic radiation. X-rays can penetrate through many kinds of solid material

BOOKS

Barr, Catherine. *Voyage Through the Solar System* (Space Voyage). Rosen Publishing Group, 2022.

DK. *Space!: The Universe as You've Never Seen it Before* (Knowledge Encyclopedia). DK Children, 2021.

Regas, Dean. *1,000 Facts about Space*. National Geographic Kids, 2023.

WEBSITES

Find out more about all aspects of our solar system at:
kids.britannica.com/students/article/solar-system/277129

Discover more about the amazing solar system at:
www.nationalgeographic.co.uk/topic/subjects/science-and-technology/space/solar-system

Watch videos and learn more about our solar system at:
www.nationalgeographic.co.uk/video/tv/solar-system-101

Publisher's note to educators and parents:
All the websites featured above have been carefully reviewed to ensure that they are suitable for students. However, many websites change often, and we cannot guarantee that a site's future contents will continue to meet our high standards of educational value. Please be advised that students should be closely monitored whenever they access the Internet.

INDEX

ABOUT THE AUTHOR

Sarah Eason has written many children's books and has a particular interest in space science. She has found researching and writing this book fascinating and hopes that it helps readers better understand the mysteries of space and maybe make it their mission to become a future space explorer.